Bible Friends
Who's Hiding?

Reader's Digest
Children's Books™

What's hiding behind the cloud?

God made everything.

Who's hiding in Noah's ark?

God kept Noah and the animals safe.

Who's hiding in the bulrushes?

God looked after Moses and kept him safe.

Who's hiding inside a big fish?

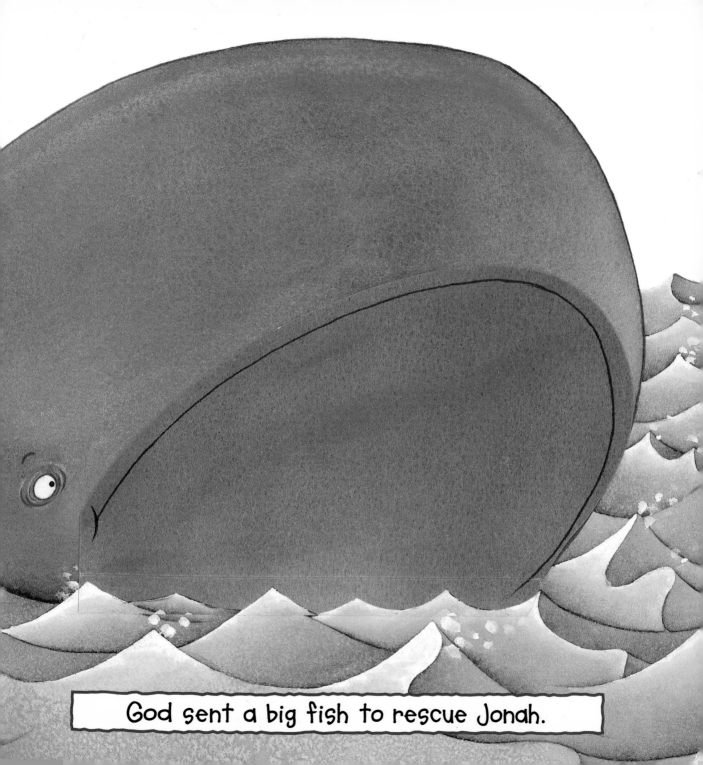

God sent a big fish to rescue Jonah.

Who's hiding behind the bush?

Jesus loves us like a good shepherd loves his sheep.

Who's hiding in the tree?

Jesus loved Zacchaeus even when no one else did.

What's hiding in the field?

a special
treasure

esus said becoming God's friend is like finding a treasure...

...it is better
than anything else
in all the world!